LET'S LEARN SOMETHING NEW!

Use at least 11 of your spelling words in a short creative story. Underline
all spelling words used in the story.

Spelling Test

Your Answers	Correct Spelling If Incorrect
1	1
2	2
3	3
4	4
5	5
6	6
7	7
8	8
9	9
10	10
11	11
12	12
13	13
14	14
15	15
16	16
17	17
18	18
19	19
20	20

5th Grade Extra Credit Spelling Words Worksheet

Name: _____

Date: _____

ashamed	amaze	century	advantage	challenge	balance
battery	century	breathe	balance	between	believe
attack	capture	behave	angrily	captain	

1. ANVATEGDA   a _ v _ _ _ _ _ _

2. AAZME   _ m _ _ _

3. LINAYRG   a _ _ r _ _ _

4. SHAEADM   _ _ h _ _ _ d

5. CATTAK   a _ _ _ _ k

6. ELNBAAC   _ a _ _ _ c _

7. CNBAEAL   b _ _ _ _ _ e

8. RTAYBET   _ a _ _ _ _ y

9. EEHVBA   _ _ _ _ v e

10. LEBEEVI   b e _ _ _ _ _

11. TEEBNEW   _ _ _ _ e _ n

12. ETAHREB   b _ e _ _ _ _

13. NAPCATI   _ _ p _ _ i _

14. PAUCTER   c _ _ _ _ r _

15. RYETNUC   _ _ n _ _ _ y

16. UNRECYT   c e _ _ _ _ _

17. EECAHGNLL   _ _ _ _ _ _ n g _

Write sentences using words from above:

1. ....

2. ....

3. ....

4. ....

Use at least 9 of your spelling words in a short creative story. Underline all spelling words used in the story.

_____

_____

_____

_____

_____

_____

_____

_____

_____

_____

_____

_____

_____

_____

_____

_____

_____

_____

_____

Spelling Test

Your Answers	Correct Spelling If Incorrect
1	1
2	2
3	3
4	4
5	5
6	6
7	7
8	8
9	9
10	10
11	11
12	12
13	13
14	14
15	15
16	16
17	17
18	18
19	19
20	20

5th Grade Extra Credit Spelling
Words Worksheet

Name: _____

Date: _____

consumer	college	charcoal	distract	correction	echo
culture	decade	churn	depth	concrete	elect
charge	computer	complain	elect	clerk	

1. LHACRCAO   _ _ _ r _ o _ _

2. EARHGC   _ h _ _ _ e

3. CRNUH   _ _ _ r _

4. ERCKL   _ _ _ _ k

5. CLGOLEE   _ _ _ l _ g _

6. PIMNALCO   _ o _ _ l _ _ _

7. PMOCTERU   _ _ m _ u _ _ _

8. CORENTCE   _ _ _ _ r _ _ e

9. SOMCREUN   c _ _ _ _ m _ _

10. TEOCIRRNCO   _ _ _ r _ c _ _ _ n

11. CUERUTL   _ _ l _ u _ _

12. DEDACE   d _ c _ _ _

13. PDETH   _ e _ _ _

14. DCASRTTI   _ _ s _ _ _ c _

15. OCEH   _ _ _ o

16. ELCET   _ _ _ c _

17. ELETC   _ l _ _ _

Write sentences using words from above:

1. ....

2. ....

3. ....

4. ....

Use at least 14 of your spelling words in a short creative story. Underline all spelling words used in the story.

Spelling Test

Your Answers		Correct Spelling If Incorrect	
1		1	
2		2	
3		3	
4		4	
5		5	
6		6	
7		7	
8		8	
9		9	
10		10	
11		11	
12		12	
13		13	
14		14	
15		15	
16		16	
17		17	
18		18	
19		19	
20		20	

5th Grade Extra Credit Spelling Words Worksheet

Name: _____

Date: _____

hangar	fortune	giraffe	evict	garden	empty
hunger	guitar	function	gracious	genius	explorer
general	heartfelt	error	hinge	gratitude	expand

1. MTPEY   _ m _ _ _

2. RERRO   e _ _ _ _

3. TEICV   _ _ _ _ t

4. AEPNXD   e _ p _ _ _

5. LEXRRPEO   _ _ p _ _ _ e _

6. EOFTURN   _ o _ _ _ n _

7. UNFCOTIN   _ u _ _ _ i _ _

8. NDRAGE   g _ _ d _ _

9. NGALEER   _ _ _ _ r _ l

10. USEING   g _ n _ _ _

11. GEFRAIF   _ _ _ _ f f _

12. UAGCSOIR   _ _ _ c _ _ u _

13. DETIRAGUT   _ r _ _ _ _ _ d _

14. URTGIA   _ _ i _ _ r

15. RNGAAH   _ _ n _ a _

16. TLETAEHFR   _ _ _ r _ f _ _ _

17. EGINH   _ _ _ _ e

18. NUHGRE   _ _ _ _ e r

Write sentences using words from above:

1. ....

2. ....

3. ....

4. ....

Use at least 7 of your spelling words in a short creative story. Underline all spelling words used in the story.

Spelling Test

Your Answers		Correct Spelling If Incorrect	
1		1	
2		2	
3		3	
4		4	
5		5	
6		6	
7		7	
8		8	
9		9	
10		10	
11		11	
12		12	
13		13	
14		14	
15		15	
16		16	
17		17	
18		18	
19		19	
20		20	

5th Grade Extra Credit Spelling Words Worksheet

Name: _____

Date: _____

initial	lotion	nerve	injure	obscure	ostrich
nonsense	ignite	pier	orchard	mansion	nominate
patient	niece	nation	longitude	lodge	nestle

1. TNIIEG   i _ n _ _ _

2. LIITAIN   _ _ _ _ _ a l

3. JRUNEI   _ n _ u _ _

4. ELGOD   _ _ _ g _

5. DNELOIUGT   _ _ _ g _ _ u _ _

6. OTLION   _ o _ _ o _

7. NANSOIM   _ a _ _ _ _ n

8. OIATNN   _ _ _ i _ n

9. EVREN   _ e _ _ _

10. NSLEET   _ _ s _ _ e

11. EICNE   _ _ e _ _

12. TEMANINO   n _ _ _ _ _ _ e

13. SSNNOEEN   _ o _ s _ _ _ _

14. ESBCORU   _ _ _ c _ r _

15. CODARRH   o _ _ h _ _ _

16. HISTCOR   o _ _ _ _ _ h

17. ETAPTIN   p _ _ _ _ n _

18. REIP   _ i _ _

Write sentences using words from above:

1. ....

2. ....

3. ....

4. ....

Use at least 8 of your spelling words in a short creative story. Underline all spelling words used in the story.

Spelling Test

Your Answers	Correct Spelling If Incorrect
1	1
2	2
3	3
4	4
5	5
6	6
7	7
8	8
9	9
10	10
11	11
12	12
13	13
14	14
15	15
16	16
17	17
18	18
19	19
20	20

5th Grade Extra Credit Spelling Words Worksheet

Name: _____

Date: _____

refrigerator	pulse	publish	rebel	remain	reason
present	punish	quarter	prong	relax	pledge
scarce	porch	precious	pondering	ratio	question

1. EPDEGL   _ _ e _ g _

2. OGINENPDR   _ _ n d _ _ _ _ _

3. RCHOP   _ _ _ c _

4. RICUOPSE   p _ _ _ _ _ s

5. NEPRTSE   _ r _ _ _ _ t

6. ONPGR   _ _ o _ _

7. BLISUHP   p _ _ l _ _ _

8. SUEPL   _ u _ _ _

9. SPNHIU   p _ _ _ s _

10. RAQETUR   q _ _ _ _ _ r

11. UTOQISEN   _ _ e _ _ i _ _

12. ORTIA   _ _ t _ _

13. AORNES   r e _ _ _ _

14. BELRE   _ _ _ e _

15. FRRIERTGEOAR   _ _ _ r _ g _ _ _ _ o _

16. EAXRL   _ _ _ a _

17. NIMREA   _ _ _ a i _

18. SACCRE   s _ _ r _ _

Write sentences using words from above:

1. _____

2. _____

3. _____

4. _____

Use at least 12 of your spelling words in a short creative story. Underline all spelling words used in the story.

_____

_____

_____

_____

_____

_____

_____

_____

_____

_____

_____

_____

_____

_____

_____

_____

_____

_____

_____

_____

Spelling Test

Your Answers		Correct Spelling If Incorrect
1	1	
2	2	
3	3	
4	4	
5	5	
6	6	
7	7	
8	8	
9	9	
10	10	
11	11	
12	12	
13	13	
14	14	
15	15	
16	16	
17	17	
18	18	
19	19	
20	20	

5th Grade Extra Credit Spelling Words Worksheet

Name: _____

Date: _____

thrash	shriveled	ultimate	signal	umbrella	vision
skiing	shimmer	spinning	thread	trendsetter	waist
spider	vacation	squeal	snagged	scorch	spread

1. OCCHRS   s _ _ _ _ h

2. SEMMRIH   _ _ _ m m _ _

3. RVSEHLEID   s _ _ i _ _ _ _ _

4. GLSANI   s _ _ _ _ l

5. KNIGSI   _ _ _ i _ g

6. SNDGEGA   s _ a _ _ _ _

7. EDSPIR   _ _ _ d e _

8. PNNIINSG   s p _ _ _ _ _ _

9. SDAREP   _ _ r _ _ d

10. ULQSAE   _ _ _ e a _

11. RTAHHS   t _ _ a _ _

12. RATHDE   _ _ r e _ _

13. ETEDESRTNTR   _ _ e _ d s _ _ _ _ _

14. UEIATLMT   _ _ _ _ m _ _ e

15. ALERUBML   _ _ b r _ _ _ _

16. ATANIVCO   v _ c _ _ _ _ _

17. SIVNOI   _ _ _ i o _

18. WTASI   _ _ _ _ t

Write sentences using words from above:

1. _____

2. _____

3. _____

4. _____

Use at least 10 of your spelling words in a short creative story. Underline all spelling words used in the story.

_____

_____

_____

_____

_____

_____

_____

_____

_____

_____

_____

_____

_____

_____

_____

_____

_____

_____

_____

Spelling Test

Your Answers		Correct Spelling If Incorrect	
1		1	
2		2	
3		3	
4		4	
5		5	
6		6	
7		7	
8		8	
9		9	
10		10	
11		11	
12		12	
13		13	
14		14	
15		15	
16		16	
17		17	
18		18	
19		19	
20		20	

5th Grade Extra Credit Spelling Words Worksheet

Name: _____

Date: _____

duet	cubic	confuse	frosted	balloon	author
awning	hawk	beauty	coleslaw	amuse	chatted
cause	bruise	alright	awfully	installation	daughter

1. TRALGHI   a _ r _ _ _ _

2. MEUAS   _ _ _ _ e

3. AOTUHR   _ u _ _ o _

4. WLYFLAU   _ _ f _ _ l _

5. NWAGNI   a _ n _ _ _

6. LNBAOOL   _ _ l _ _ _ n

7. BUYAET   _ _ a _ t _

8. SERUBI   _ _ u i _ _

9. AUSEC   _ _ _ s _

10. HTDCAET   _ _ _ _ _ e d

11. EASCLWLO   c _ l _ _ _ _ _

12. UNFESOC   c _ _ _ u _ _

13. IUCCB   _ _ _ i _

14. URTEHAGD   d _ _ g _ _ _ _

15. TDUE   _ _ e _

16. DFROETS   _ r _ s _ _ _

17. KHWΛ   _ a _ _

18. ILTAALTIONNS   i _ _ _ _ l _ a _ _ _ _

Write sentences using words from above:

1. ....

2. ....

3. ....

4. ....

Use at least 5 of your spelling words in a short creative story. Underline all spelling words used in the story.

Spelling Test

Your Answers	Correct Spelling If Incorrect
1	1
2	2
3	3
4	4
5	5
6	6
7	7
8	8
9	9
10	10
11	11
12	12
13	13
14	14
15	15
16	16
17	17
18	18
19	19
20	20

5th Grade Extra Credit Spelling Words Worksheet

Name: _____

Date: _____

pursue	scrawny	nephew	laundry	vacuum	unicorn
unit	issue	lawful	sauce	usually	peruse
preferred	value	mutation	unicycle	musical	taught

1. ISUES   _ s _ _ _

2. AUDNRYL   _ _ _ n _ r _

3. LFUWLA   _ _ _ f _ l

4. MSUIACL   m u _ _ _ _ _

5. AUTITNOM   m _ _ a _ _ _ _

6. NWEPEH   n _ _ _ e _

7. RPSEUE   p _ r _ _ _

8. EERRDERPF   _ _ _ f e _ _

9. URSUEP   _ u r _ _ _

10. AEUSC   _ _ u _ _

11. CRSWNYA   _ c _ a _ _ _

12. UGTTAH   _ a _ _ _ t

13. NICONUR   u _ _ _ _ _ n

14. IYECLUCN   _ n _ _ y _ _ _

15. IUNT   u _ _ _

16. UYLLAUS   u _ _ _ _ _ y

17. LIVMACU   _ _ _ u _ m

18. EAVLU   _ _ _ _ e

Write sentences using words from above:

1. ....

2. ....

3. ....

4. ....

Use at least 16 of your spelling words in a short creative story. Underline all spelling words used in the story.

_____

_____

_____

_____

_____

_____

_____

_____

_____

_____

_____

_____

_____

_____

_____

_____

_____

_____

_____

_____

Spelling Test

Your Answers		Correct Spelling If Incorrect	
1		1	
2		2	
3		3	
4		4	
5		5	
6		6	
7		7	
8		8	
9		9	
10		10	
11		11	
12		12	
13		13	
14		14	
15		15	
16		16	
17		17	
18		18	
19		19	
20		20	

Use at least 14 of your spelling words in a short creative story. Underline all spelling words used in the story.

Spelling Test

Your Answers		Correct Spelling If Incorrect
1	1	
2	2	
3	3	
4	4	
5	5	
6	6	
7	7	
8	8	
9	9	
10	10	
11	11	
12	12	
13	13	
14	14	
15	15	
16	16	
17	17	
18	18	
19	19	
20	20	

Use at least 17 of your spelling words in a short creative story. Underline all spelling words used in the story.

Spelling Test

Your Answers	Correct Spelling If Incorrect
1	1
2	2
3	3
4	4
5	5
6	6
7	7
8	8
9	9
10	10
11	11
12	12
13	13
14	14
15	15
16	16
17	17
18	18
19	19
20	20

Use at least 5 of your spelling words in a short creative story. Underline all spelling words used in the story.

_____

_____

_____

_____

_____

_____

_____

_____

_____

_____

_____

_____

_____

_____

_____

_____

_____

_____

_____

Spelling Test

Your Answers	Correct Spelling If Incorrect
1	1
2	2
3	3
4	4
5	5
6	6
7	7
8	8
9	9
10	10
11	11
12	12
13	13
14	14
15	15
16	16
17	17
18	18
19	19
20	20

Use at least 7 of your spelling words in a short creative story. Underline all spelling words used in the story.

Spelling Test

Your Answers		Correct Spelling If Incorrect	
1		1	
2		2	
3		3	
4		4	
5		5	
6		6	
7		7	
8		8	
9		9	
10		10	
11		11	
12		12	
13		13	
14		14	
15		15	
16		16	
17		17	
18		18	
19		19	
20		20	

Use at least 12 of your spelling words in a short creative story. Underline all spelling words used in the story.

Spelling Test

Your Answers	Correct Spelling If Incorrect
1	1
2	2
3	3
4	4
5	5
6	6
7	7
8	8
9	9
10	10
11	11
12	12
13	13
14	14
15	15
16	16
17	17
18	18
19	19
20	20

Use at least 10 of your spelling words in a short creative story. Underline all spelling words used in the story.

Spelling Test

Your Answers		Correct Spelling If Incorrect
1		1
2		2
3		3
4		4
5		5
6		6
7		7
8		8
9		9
10		10
11		11
12		12
13		13
14		14
15		15
16		16
17		17
18		18
19		19
20		20

Use at least 8 of your spelling words in a short creative story. Underline all spelling words used in the story.

Spelling Test

Your Answers	Correct Spelling If Incorrect
1	1
2	2
3	3
4	4
5	5
6	6
7	7
8	8
9	9
10	10
11	11
12	12
13	13
14	14
15	15
16	16
17	17
18	18
19	19
20	20

Use at least 13 of your spelling words in a short creative story. Underline all spelling words used in the story.

Spelling Test

Your Answers	Correct Spelling If Incorrect
1	1
2	2
3	3
4	4
5	5
6	6
7	7
8	8
9	9
10	10
11	11
12	12
13	13
14	14
15	15
16	16
17	17
18	18
19	19
20	20

Use at least 11 of your spelling words in a short creative story. Underline all spelling words used in the story.

Spelling Test

Your Answers	Correct Spelling If Incorrect
1	1
2	2
3	3
4	4
5	5
6	6
7	7
8	8
9	9
10	10
11	11
12	12
13	13
14	14
15	15
16	16
17	17
18	18
19	19
20	20

Use at least 9 of your spelling words in a short creative story. Underline all spelling words used in the story.

Spelling Test

Your Answers		Correct Spelling If Incorrect	
1		1	
2		2	
3		3	
4		4	
5		5	
6		6	
7		7	
8		8	
9		9	
10		10	
11		11	
12		12	
13		13	
14		14	
15		15	
16		16	
17		17	
18		18	
19		19	
20		20	

Use at least 15 of your spelling words in a short creative story. Underline all spelling words used in the story.

Use at least 11 of your spelling words in a short creative story. Underline all spelling words used in the story.

Spelling Test

Your Answers	**Correct Spelling If Incorrect**
1	1
2	2
3	3
4	4
5	5
6	6
7	7
8	8
9	9
10	10
11	11
12	12
13	13
14	14
15	15
16	16
17	17
18	18
19	19
20	20

Use at least 9 of your spelling words in a short creative story. Underline all spelling words used in the story.

_____

_____

_____

_____

_____

_____

_____

_____

_____

_____

_____

_____

_____

_____

_____

_____

_____

_____

_____

Spelling Test

Your Answers

1 _____
2 _____
3 _____
4 _____
5 _____
6 _____
7 _____
8 _____
9 _____
10 _____
11 _____
12 _____
13 _____
14 _____
15 _____
16 _____
17 _____
18 _____
19 _____
20

Correct Spelling If Incorrect

1 _____
2 _____
3 _____
4 _____
5 _____
6 _____
7 _____
8 _____
9 _____
10 _____
11 _____
12 _____
13 _____
14 _____
15 _____
16 _____
17 _____
18 _____
19 _____
20

Use at least 14 of your spelling words in a short creative story. Underline all spelling words used in the story.

Spelling Test

Your Answers		Correct Spelling If Incorrect
1	1
2	2
3	3
4	4
5	5
6	6
7	7
8	8
9	9
10	10
11	11
12	12
13	13
14	14
15	15
16	16
17	17
18	18
19	19
20	20

Class: _____

		Week or Month:_____					Week or Month:_____					Week or Month:_____					Week or Month:_____				
Day																								
Date																								
Assignments																								
Name																								
	1																							
	2																							
	3																							
	4																							
	5																							
	6																							
	7																							
	8																							
	9																							
	10																							
	11																							
	12																							
	13																							
	14																							
	15																							
	16																							
	17																							
	18																							
	19																							
	20																							
	21																							
	22																							
	23																							
	24																							
	25																							
	26																							
	27																							
	28																							
	29																							
	30																							
	31																							
	32																							

Class: _____

		Week or Month:_____					Week or Month:_____					Week or Month:_____					Week or Month:_____				
Day																							
Date																							
Assignments																							
Name																							
	1																						
	2																						
	3																						
	4																						
	5																						
	6																						
	7																						
	8																						
	9																						
	10																						
	11																						
	12																						
	13																						
	14																						
	15																						
	16																						
	17																						
	18																						
	19																						
	20																						
	21																						
	22																						
	23																						
	24																						
	25																						
	26																						
	27																						
	28																						
	29																						
	30																						
	31																						
	32																						